# PARÈS SCALES

### For Individual Study
### and Like-Instrument Class Instruction

*by* **GABRIEL PARÈS**

**Revised and Edited by Harvey S. Whistler**

## Published for:

Flute or Piccolo . . . . . . . . . . . . . . . . . . . . . . Parès-Whistler

Clarinet . . . . . . . . . . . . . . . . . . . . . . . . . Parès-Whistler

Oboe . . . . . . . . . . . . . . . . . . . . . . . . . . . Parès-Whistler

Bassoon . . . . . . . . . . . . . . . . . . . . . . . . . Parès-Whistler

Saxophone . . . . . . . . . . . . . . . . . . . . . . . . Parès-Whistler

Cornet, Trumpet or Baritone 𝄞 . . . . . . . . . . . . Parès-Whistler

French Horn, E♭ Alto or Mellophone . . . . . . . . Parès-Whistler

Trombone or Baritone 𝄢 . . . . . . . . . . . . . . Parès-Whistler

E♭ Bass . . . . . . . . . . . . . . . . . . . . . . . . . Parès-Whistler

BB♭ Bass . . . . . . . . . . . . . . . . . . . . . . . . Parès-Whistler

Marimba, Xylophone or Vibes . . . . . . . Parès-Whistler-Jolliff

**For Individual Study and Like-Instrument Class Instruction**
**(Not Playable by Bands or by Mixed-Instruments)**

**RUBANK**®

**HAL•LEONARD**®
**CORPORATION**
7777 W. BLUEMOUND RD. P.O. BOX 13819 MILWAUKEE, WI 53213

L-123

# Key of C Major
## Long Rolls to Strengthen Wrists

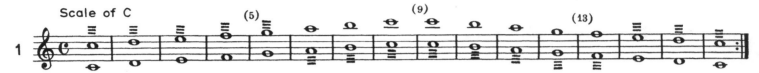

Also practice rolling each tone for EIGHT counts.
When playing the rolls, practice: (1) `<` and (2) `<  >`.
Alternate the mallets.  Do not cross the mallets. Practice each exercise starting first with the left mallet and then with the right.

1011 - 45

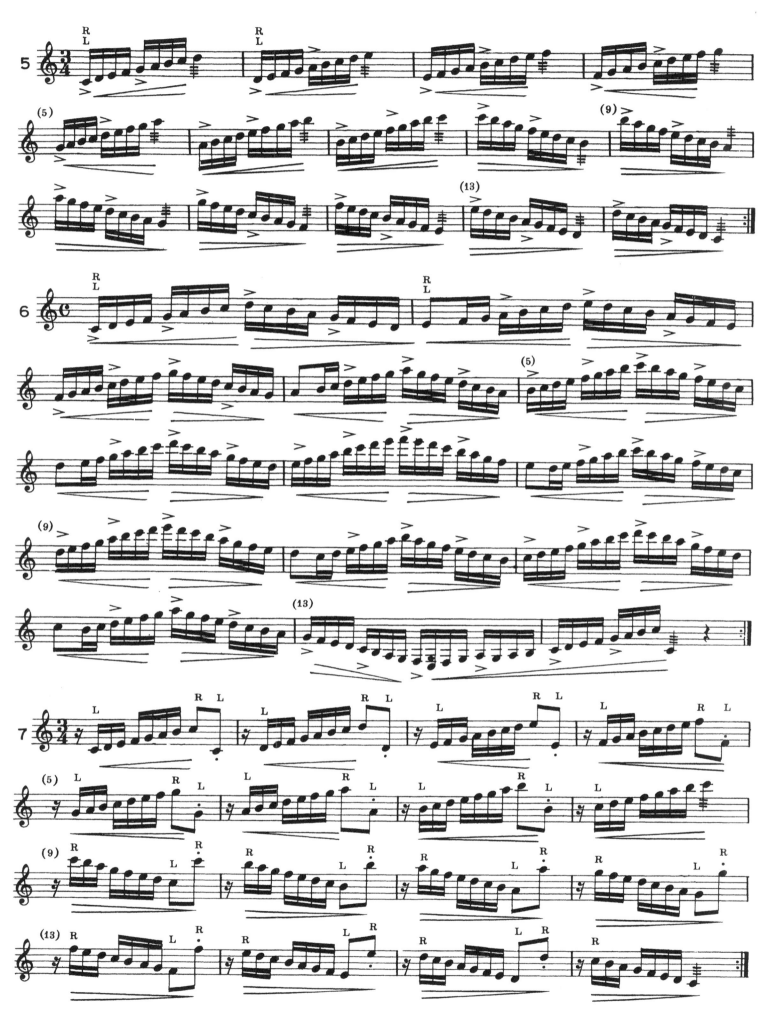

## Developing the Roll

# Key of G Major

## Long Rolls to Strengthen Wrists

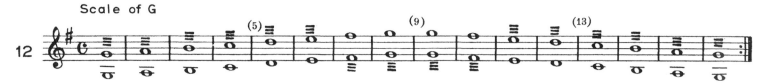

**12**

Also practice rolling each tone for EIGHT counts.
When playing the rolls, practice: (1) ⤙ and (2) ⤙⤚.
Alternate the mallets. Do not cross the mallets. Practice each exercise starting first with
the left mallet and then with the right.

Developing the Roll

# Key of F Major

## Long Rolls to Strengthen Wrists

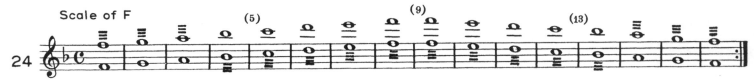

Also practice rolling each tone for EIGHT counts.
When playing the rolls, practice: (1) $<$ and (2) $< >$
Alternate the mallets.  Do not cross the mallets. Practice each exercise starting first with
the left mallet and then with the right.

8

This study may also be played an octave lower

etc.

## Developing the Roll

# Key of D Major

## Long Rolls to Strengthen Wrists

Also practice rolling each tone for EIGHT counts.
When playing the rolls, practice: (1) ⤙ and (2) ⤙ ⤚.
Alternate the mallets. Do not cross the mallets. Practice each exercise starting first with the left mallet and then with the right.

## Developing the Roll

# Key of B♭ Major

## Long Rolls to Strengthen Wrists

Also practice rolling each tone for EIGHT counts.

When playing the rolls, practice: (1) $\leq$ and (2) $\leq$ $\geq$.

Alternate the mallets. Do not cross the mallets. Practice each exercise starting first with the left mallet and then with the right.

## Developing the Roll

# Key of A Major

## Long Rolls to Strengthen Wrists

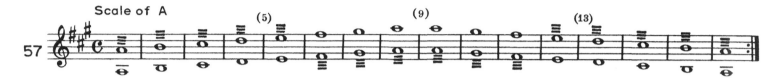

Also practice rolling each tone for EIGHT counts.
When playing the rolls, practice: (1) ⏗ and (2) ⏗⏘.
Alternate the mallets. Do not cross the mallets. Practice each exercise starting first with
the left mallet and then with the right.

18

## Developing the Roll

# Key of E♭ Major

## Long Rolls to Strengthen Wrists

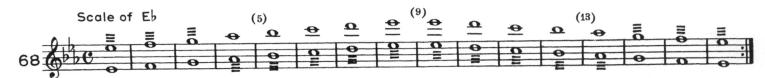

Also practice rolling each tone for EIGHT counts.
When playing the rolls, practice: (1) ≺ and (2) ≺≻.
Alternate the mallets. Do not cross the mallets. Practice each exercise starting first with
the left mallet and then with the right.

## Developing the Roll

# Key of E Major

## Long Rolls to Strengthen Wrists

Also practice rolling each tone for EIGHT counts.
When playing the rolls, practice: (1) ⬍ and (2) ⬍.
Alternate the mallets. Do not cross the mallets. Practice each exercise starting first with
the left mallet and then with the right.

*This study may also be played an octave lower*

24

## Developing the Roll

# Key of A♭ Major

## Long Rolls to Strengthen Wrists

Also practice rolling each tone for EIGHT counts.
When playing the rolls, practice: (1) ⟨ and (2) ⟨ ⟩.
Alternate the mallets. Do not cross the mallets. Practice each exercise starting first with
the left mallet and then with the right.

### Developing the Roll

# Key of A Minor

### (Relative to the Key of C Major)

## Long Rolls to Strengthen Wrists

Also practice rolling each tone for EIGHT counts.
When playing the rolls, practice: (1) ‹ and (2) ‹ ›.
Alternate the mallets. Do not cross the mallets. Practice each exercise starting first with
the left mallet and then with the right.

## Developing the Roll

# Key of E Minor

(Relative to the Key of G Major)

## Long Rolls to Strengthen Wrists

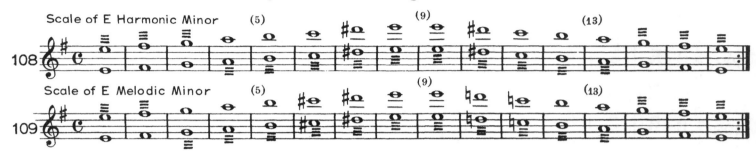

Also practice rolling each tone for EIGHT counts.
When playing the rolls, practice: (1) ⬿ and (2) ⬿⬾.
Alternate the mallets. Do not cross the mallets. Practice each exercise starting first with
the left mallet and then with the right.

## Developing the Roll

# Key of D Minor

(Relative to the Key of F Major)

## Long Rolls to Strengthen Wrists

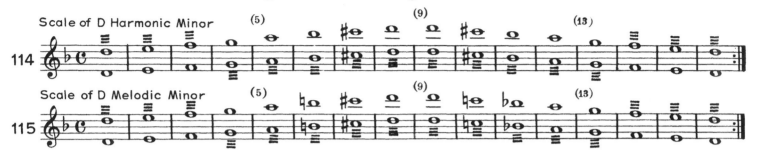

Also practice rolling each tone for EIGHT counts.
When playing the rolls, practice: (1) ⟨ and (2) ⟨ ⟩.
Alternate the mallets. Do not cross the mallets. Practice each exercise starting first, with the left mallet and then with the right.

## Developing the Roll

# Key of B Minor

(Relative to the Key of D Major)

## Long Rolls to Strengthen Wrists

Scale of B Harmonic Minor

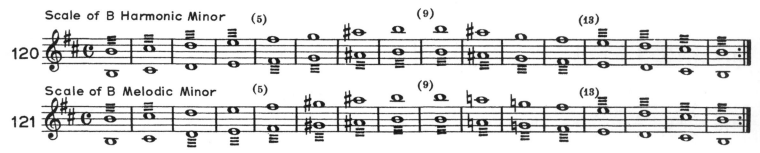

Also practice rolling each tone for EIGHT counts.
When playing the rolls, practice: (1) ⟨ and (2) ⟨ ⟩.
Alternate the mallets. Do not cross the mallets. Practice each exercise starting first with the left mallet and then with the right.

## Developing the Roll

# Key of G Minor
### (Relative to the Key of B♭ Major)

## Long Rolls to Strengthen Wrists

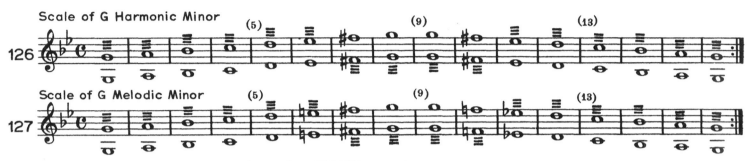

Also practice rolling each tone for EIGHT counts.
When playing the rolls, practice: (1) ⎯⎯ and (2) ⎯⎯⎯.
Alternate the mallets. Do not cross the mallets. Practice each exercise starting first with the left mallet and then with the right.

## Developing the Roll

# Key of F# Minor

(Relative to the Key of A Major)

## Long Rolls to Strengthen Wrists

Also practice rolling each tone for EIGHT counts.

When playing the rolls, practice: (1) ⟨ and (2) ⟨ ⟩

Alternate the mallets. Do not cross the mallets. Practice each exercise starting first with the left mallet and then with the right.

## Developing the Roll

# Key of C Minor
### (Relative to the Key of E♭ Major)
## Long Rolls to Strengthen Wrists

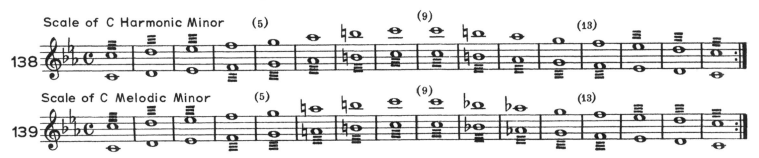

Also practice rolling each tone for EIGHT counts.

When playing the rolls, practice: (1) $\longleftarrow$ and (2) $\longleftarrow \longrightarrow$ .

Alternate the mallets.  Do not cross the mallets. Practice each exercise starting first with the left mallet and then with the right.

## Developing the Roll

# Key of C♯ Minor
### (Relative to the Key of E Major)

## Long Rolls to Strengthen Wrists

Scale of C♯ Harmonic Minor

**144**

Scale of C♯ Melodic Minor

**145**

Also practice rolling each tone for EIGHT counts.
When playing the rolls, practice: (1) ⟍⟋ and (2) ⟍⟋⟍.
Alternate the mallets.  Do not cross the mallets. Practice each exercise starting first with
the left mallet and then with the right.

**146**

**147**

## Developing the Roll

**148**

**149**

# Key of F Minor
(Relative to the Key of A♭ Major)

## Long Rolls to Strengthen Wrists

Also practice rolling each tone for EIGHT counts.

When playing the rolls, practice: (1) ⟨ and (2) ⟨⟩.

Alternate the mallets. Do not cross the mallets. Practice each exercise starting first with the left mallet and then with the right.

## Developing the Roll

# Major Scales

# Harmonic Minor Scales

# Melodic Minor Scales

# Arpeggios

# Chromatic Scales

## Two Octave Chromatic Scales

# Scales in Thirds

# Studies in Sixths

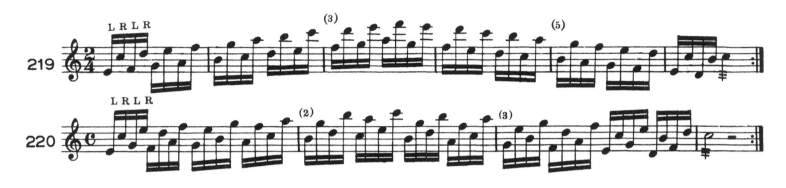

## Combined Thirds and Sixths

## Triplet Study

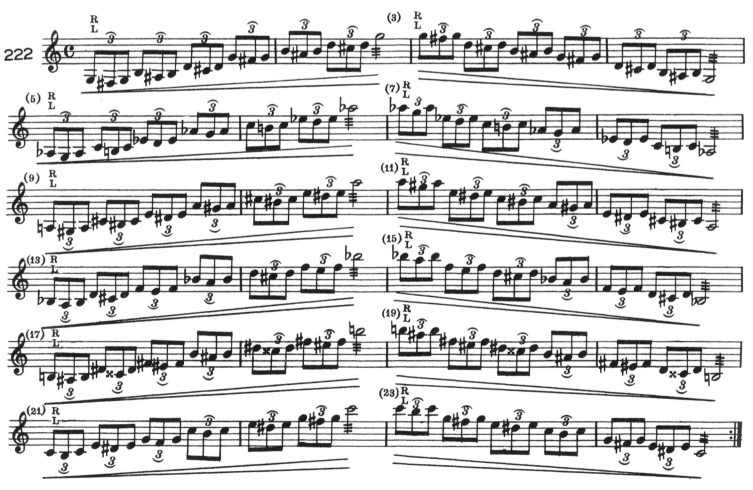

# Octave Study